LIFE'S HIGHWAY

The Choices We Make

Russ Myers

Table of Contents

ACKNOWLEDGEMENTS

Special thanks to:

Dr. Dave Bryan is a close friend and pastor of 28 years at Chisholm Heights Baptist Church and a Southern Baptist Executive Committee member.

Ryan Churchill for his artistic talent.

Elise Barger for her review and questions.

Jason Myers my son with his master's degree in theological education and his questions and discussion on the impact of this paper.

Aaron Myers is my son and one of the most faithful people to God's leading in his life.

Janis Myers, my wife of 53 years and her love and care for me.

John Myers my father is one of the most knowledgeable laymen of the bible you can ever meet. He is still thinking about this paper as fathers would be.

Many other pastors and friends have had an impact on me.

Bible Study Fellowship (BSF) in Oklahoma City

FOREWARD

Hello, I am now 70-something years of age and would like to tell you about the "Life's Highway" that I have been on. There have been many intersections (decisions) that have been made—both good and bad—as you will find out in this book.

The first and most important thing to know about is the decision I made when I was eight years old to accept Christ as my Lord and Savior. At eight there is not much happening in your life, but one day a friend and I were walking home from school on the railroad tracks when two men stopped us and said that it was against the law to walk on the tracks, and they would have to report the violation to our parents. It happens that our church was in a revival that week and the preacher by the name of Johnnie Bisagno was there and said that God would forgive you for your sins. That was all I needed to hear because I had sinned and broken the law and needed God's forgiveness and protection. Being only eight your life doesn't change a lot when you get saved. Life went on and I was a good kid (well I think so) but didn't grow in the Lord's way. I attended church and Bible study but was not very engaged. There were too many other things that had my attention, sports mostly.

In high school, I met a young lady who became my wife. She was raised Catholic, and I was Baptist. I visited her church and asked her to come to my church. She came and accepted Jesus as her personal Savior which has turned out to be the best thing that could have happened to her and me. She has been the most encouraging for my walk with God for many years.

We had a son after we had been married for three years. The first three years were difficult because of my turning away from the Lord. I will discuss this later in the book and how it formed some of the thoughts I now express about the highway my life has taken...

Two years after our son was born, we had another child. It was a precious little girl. She was prematurely born and had many physical issues. She passed away two months after she was born. Looking back at this time, I can only say that God was carrying me on his shoulders through the storm. This is the impetus for this book and the questions and answers that I propose, and I have come to believe how the Bible addresses each.

The first thing that we must do when we have questions of God is to search his Word. So, I have done an exhaustive search in the Bible about what the answers are to the following questions I would like to put before you.

1. When does Jesus (God) know me?
2. Do babies who die, aborted, or miscarried go to Heaven?
3. How is the age of accountability determined?
4. Do we have a choice to be saved? Is there a time limit to make the choice?
5. What does "Life's Highway" consist of or mean?
6. Will God shorten or lengthen your time here?
7. What will be the final results of your life?
8. What is God's Will for you and me?
9. What does "predestination" mean?

I would ask that you spend much time in thought and prayer when reading these concepts. Use all the spiritual discernment that you have. Thoughts and prayers are easily explained but let me spend a moment on spiritual discernment. You can only have spiritual discernment if you know Jesus as your Savior and discernment doesn't happen immediately.

As you grow in the knowledge of Christ you can recognize (discern) different things in the Bible. God helps you understand what you are reading. The scriptures are new each time I read them. God always has something to say to me. Jesus taught in parables so that those that didn't believe in Him would not understand the full meaning.

So, please take time to think about these ideas; pray about them and discern with God's help what is being proposed to you here. You may agree with some or none and that is okay. God does not provide the full explanation of many things in the Bible. It is a book about His Son and the salvation he brings to the world, not a science book.

For example, I have many Christian brothers and sisters that do not agree on the tribulation period and what is going to happen at that time. But that is okay. Many books have been written on the subject and there is still a lot of disagreement. God will answer all questions soon. I am not going to discuss the tribulation period in this book.

Before I start discussing these questions in depth, it is more important that you know Christ as your personal Savior. It is a simple decision, just in my testimony above. You need to realize that you have sinned and only because of Jesus' sacrifice and resurrection can you have eternal life in Heaven with God and your loved ones. Choosing to believe in Jesus is the most important thing you can do. If you have not prayed and asked God to forgive you and accept the gift of Christ as your Savior, please do so now before it is too late.

CHAPTER ONE

THE BOOK OF LIFE

The most important question is: what is 'the Book of Life?'

In Revelations chapter 20, verse 12, "And I saw the dead, the great and the small, standing before the throne, and books were opened; and another book was opened, which is the Book of Life; and the dead were judged from the things which were written in the books, according to their deeds."

God has two sets of books. One of the lost (Judgment) is those that have not chosen to accept Christ. The second is the list of names of those who have accepted the Saving Grace of God through Jesus Christ.

Book One (Judgment) is the list of names and deeds (sins) that the lost are guilty of doing and they now face judgment to pay the price for these deeds.

We all must pay the price for our sins.

Romans 6:23, *"For the wages of sin is death, but the gift of God is eternal life in Christ Jesus our Lord."*

There is a price to pay for our sins in this world. We must pay for the debts of our sins. So, how do we pay the debt? What is the judgment for the sins we have committed? The price or payment we would pay is separation from God. When someone dies separated from God, they will spend eternity in Hell. I can only imagine that there is a big-screen television showing the lives of everyone listed in this book. I would not want my life to be shown on this screen.

It only takes one sin to condemn us to Hell and that is the rejection of Jesus as your personal Savior. The Bible outlines numerous sins, that is sexual immorality, murder, idolatry, hatred, envy, etc.. I venture to say that no one only has one sin. Even if you had only one sin and have not accepted Jesus you will go to Hell. You cannot be good enough; you can't do enough good things; or you can't give enough money to pay the price for your sins.

Ephesians 2:8-9, *"For it is by grace you have been saved, through faith-and this is not from yourselves, it is the gift of God- not by works so that no one can boast."*

So, what is the big deal about being separated from God for eternity? The Devil has people thinking it will be a party but that is not the case. Jesus describes Hell in **Matthew 13:49,** *"So it will be at the end of the age; the angles will come forth and take out the wicked from among the righteous and will throw them into the furnace of fire; in that place, there will be weeping and gnashing of teeth."*

When you reach the end of God's Grace, nothing is left but God's wrath. This is not a party I would want to attend, and you shouldn't either because you will be alone. You see, in the Bible, time and time again where God judges His people (Israel) and sends them into captivity of another nation. That is because they ignore God's message to them to repent and turn to Him for forgiveness. Read Jeremiah for one example.

The second book is the Book of Life. We know that the names listed in this book are those who have accepted Jesus Christ as their savior. The apostle, John, wrote in **Revelations 21: 27**, *"And nothing unclean, and no one who practices abomination and lying, shall ever come into it, but only those whose names are written in the Lamb's Book of Life."*

John is talking about entering God's presence or Heaven. What about the list of deeds and sins of those listed in this book? Our sins have been paid for by Jesus' sacrifice on the cross and therefore they (sins) are not listed. God forgives and forgets our sins. All our past, present, and future sins. Psalms 103:12 "As far as the east is from the west, so far has he removed our transgressions from us." 1 John 1:7 "and the blood of Jesus, his Son, purifies us from all sin." God has the book of our names. I believe that our names as Christians and the deeds that we have done for God will be listed. This will determine what our crown of glory looks like. We will not care about the crown because we will be in the presence of God.

The Book of Life is mentioned as early as Exodus when the Lord replied to Moses, "Whoever has sinned against me I will blot out of my book. (Which refers to the Book of Life). We read about the Book of Life throughout the Bible and at the end of Revelations 20: 15 where we see anyone whose name is not found written in the Book of Life was thrown into the lake of fire, Revelation 13:8, and so on.

Okay, there are different books, so when do the names get listed in the books? I have talked about why they are listed in the books. Now I will give you my thoughts regarding when our names are listed in each of these books.

CHAPTER TWO

WHEN & WHICH BOOK ARE YOU IN?

In Ephesians 1:4 "for he chose us in Him before the creation of the world to be holy and blameless in his sight, in love." There are many instances you can read in the Bible that God knew someone before they were born.

In Isaiah 45:1, we read Cyrus King of Persia was named by Isaiah about 150 years before he was born. You will read that God gave names to John the Baptist (Luke 1:13), and Jeremiah (Jeremiah 1:4-5) before their birth. So, God must have the list in place and knows the future of each person.

In Psalms 139: 13-16 David writes – "For you created my inmost being: you knit me together in my mother's womb. I praise you because I am fearfully and wonderfully made; your works are wonderful; I know that full well. My frame was not hidden from you when I was made in the secret place. When I was woven together in the depths of the earth. Your eyes saw my unformed body and all the days ordained for me were **written in your book before one of them came to be.**"

The first assumption that I make regarding when our names are written in the Book of Life in Heaven is: **I believe that all people's names are listed in the book from the creation of the world as stated in Ephesians**. Why do I think this?

II Peter 3:9 "The Lord is not slow about His promise, as some count slowness, but is patient toward you, not willing for any to perish, but for all to come to repentance". If it is true, **God wants all to be saved** and it is because God is incapable of lying. My assumption that we are listed in the Book of Life means we all have a chance to choose to accept the call to Jesus as our savior. When you make that choice to accept the call to Jesus then your name becomes permanently listed in the Book of Life. Like the notary seal that verifies your signature, **the blood of Christ seals your name in the book**. If you die after the age of accountability, never having chosen to accept Jesus, then your name is erased from the Book of Life. We will discuss the age of accountability later.

This assumption is contrary to what I have heard from preachers throughout my life. The statement that they have made is generally, when you are saved your name is then written in the Book of Life. Because of these statements by many respected pastors, I set out to disprove my thoughts about when we are listed in the Book of Life or the first books of judgment.

Let's examine what the Scriptures say about when your name is being "written in the Book of Life".

Our first-time hearing about the Book of Life is in Exodus 32:31-33. So, Moses went back to the LORD and said, "Oh, what a great sin these people have committed! They have made themselves gods of gold. But now, please forgive their sin – but if not, then **blot me out of the book you have written**." The LORD replied to Moses, "Whoever has sinned against me **I will blot out of my book**".

II Kings 14:26-27 "The LORD had seen how bitterly everyone in Israel, whether slave or free, was suffering; there was no one to help them. And since the **LORD had not said he would blot out the name of Israel from under Heaven**, he saved them by the hand of Jeroboam son of Jehoash."

Luke 10:20 "However, do not rejoice that the spirits submit to you, but rejoice that your names are written in Heaven."

Revelations 3:5, "*He who overcomes will, like them, be dressed in white. I will never blot out his name from the Book of Life but will acknowledge his name before my Father and his angels.*"

Revelations 17:8, "*The beast, which you saw, once was, now is not, and will come up out of the Abyss and go to his destruction. The inhabitants of the earth whose names have not been written in the Book of Life from the creation of the world will be astonished when they see the beast, because he once was, now is not, and yet will come.*"

In this verse we see that there are **names that have not continued to remain written in the Book of Life**, these names are those that have been blotted out.

We see from the verse in Revelations and Ephesians that God started writing the names when the world was created.

We also know that God is very detail oriented based on his creation. So, if we follow the logic (this is man's logic) we can make some assumptions from the Scriptures.

1. God wrote our names in the Book of Life when he created the world. Psalms 139:16

2. We all have a choice to make regarding His call to salvation through Christ Jesus.

3. If we reject his call of salvation through Christ and we do not have any future opportunities to make the choice (a hardened heart), then your name will be blotted out of the Book of Life.

4. We don't know how many chances we have to make the choice, only God does.

5. If your name gets blotted out of the Book of Life, it is transferred to the other book of judgment with your list of sins.

6. If a baby or a person is unable to understand or has no power of reasoning to decide, then God's grace covers them. They are unable to make a choice. Discussed in the next chapter.

CHAPTER THREE

BEFORE THE AGE
OF ACCOUNTABILITY - BABIES

Let's assume I am correct, and that God lists everyone in the Book of Life at the creation of the world. That means everyone's name is in the book and only the choice to not accept the call to Jesus as a personal savior moves your name from the Book of Life to the Book of Judgment. Then what do believe about babies and those that are unable to make a choice? Where do they fit into this equation?

Let's first hear what has been said by our theologians and how they have explained why children are in Heaven.

R. Albert Mohler, Jr. and Daniel L. Akin wrote a paper about this entitled "Why we believe young children who die go to Heaven." This was what I heard and still hear but it just doesn't seem to be a complete answer.

Why do we believe young children who die go to Heaven?

Few things in life are more tragic and heartbreaking than the death of a baby or small child. For parents, the grief can be overwhelming. For the minister, to stand over a small, white casket and provide comfort and support seems to ask for more than he can deliver.

Many console themselves with the thought that at least the child is now in a better place. Some believe small children who die become angels. They are certain these precious little ones are in Heaven with God.

However, we both need to ask and answer some important questions if we can. Do those who die in infancy go to Heaven? How do we know" what evidence is there to support such a conclusion? Sentimentalism and emotional hopes and wants are not sufficient for those who live under the authority of the Word of God. We must, if possible, find out what God has said.

It is interesting to discover that the Church has not been of one mind on this issue. The early and medieval Church was anything but united. Some church fathers remained silent on the issue.

Ambrose said unbaptized infants were not admitted to Heaven but had immunity from the pains of Hell.

Augustine affirmed the damnation of all unbaptized infants but taught they would receive the mildest punishment of all.

Gregory of Nyssa offed that infants who die immediately mature and are allowed to trust Christ.

Calvin affirmed the certain election of some infants to salvation and was open to the possibility that all infants who die are saved. He said, "Christ receives not only those, moved by holy desire and faith freely approach not Him, but those who are not yet of age to know how much they need His grace."

Zqingli, B.B. Warfield, and Charles Hodge all taught that God saves all who die in infancy. This perspective has basically become the dominant view of the Church in the 20th century.

Yet, a popular evangelical theologian chided Billy Graham when at the Oklahoma City memorial service, he said, "Someday there will be a glorious reunion with those who have died and gone to Heaven before us, and that includes all those innocent children that are lost. They're not lost from God because any child that young is automatically in Heaven and in God's arms" The theologian scolded Graham for offering what he called" …a new gospel: justification by youth alone."

It is our conviction that there are good reasons biblically and theologically for believing that God saves all who die who do not reach a stage of moral understanding and accountability. It is readily admitted that Scripture does not speak to the issue directly, yet there is evidence that can be gleaned that would lead us to affirm on biblical grounds that God receives into Heaven all who have died in infancy. Some evidence is stronger than others, but cumulatively they marshal strong support for infant salvation. We will note six of them.

First, the grace, goodness and mercy of God would support the position that God saves all infants who die. This is the strongest argument and perhaps the decisive one. God is love (1 John 4:8) and desires that all be saved (I Timothy 2:4). God is love and His concern for children is evident in Matthew 18:14 where Jesus says, "your Father in Heaven is not willing that any of these little ones should be lost." People go to Hell because they choose in willful rebellion and unbelief to reject God and His grace. Children are incapable of this kind of conscious rejection of God. Where such rebellion and willful disobedience is absent, God is gracious to receive.

Second, when a baby boy who was born to David and Bathsheba died (2 Samuel 12:15-18), David did two significant things: 1) He confessed his confidence that he would see the child again and, 2) he comforted his wife Bathsheba (vs23-24). David could have done those two things only if he was confident that his little son was with God. Any other explanation does not do justice to the text.

Third, in James 4:17, the Bible says, "To one who knows the good he ought to do and doesn't do it, it is sin for them." The Bible is clear that we are all born with a sinful nature because of being in Adam (Romans 5:12). This is what is called the doctrine of original sin. However, the

Scriptures make a distinction between original sin and actual sins. While all are guilty of original sin, moral responsibility, and understanding are necessary for our being accountable for actual sins (Deuteronomy 1:30; Isaiah 7:16). It is to the one who knows to do right and does not do it that sin is reckoned. Infants and some that have a mental disability are incapable of such decisions.

Fourth, Jesus affirmed that the kingdom of God belonged to little children (Luke 18:15-17). In the passage, he is stating that saving faith is a childlike faith, but He also seems to be affirming the reality of children populating Heaven.

Fifth, Scripture affirms that the number of saved souls is very great (Revelation 7:9). Since most of the world has been and is still non-Christian, might it be the untold multitude who have died prematurely or in infancy comprise a majority of those in Heaven? Such a possibility ought not to be dismissed too quickly. In this context, Charles Spurgeon said, "I rejoice to know that the souls of all infants, as soon as they die, speed their way to paradise. Think what a multitude there is of them".

Sixth, some in Scripture are said to be chosen or sanctified from the womb (1 Samuel 1:8-2:21; Jeremiah 1:5; Luke 1:15). This certainly affirms the salvation of some infants and repudiates the view that only baptized babies are assured of Heaven. Neither Samuel, Jeremiah, nor John the Baptist was baptized.

After surveying these arguments, we need to remember that anyone who is saved is saved because of the grace of God, the saving work of Jesus Christ, and the undeserved and unmerited regenerating work of the Holy Spirit. Like all who have ever lived, except for Jesus, infants need to be saved. Only Jesus can take away their sin, and if they are saved it is because of His sovereign grace and abounding mercy.

Abraham said, "Will not the Judge of all the earth do, right?" (Genesis 18:25). We can confidently say, "Yes, He will." When it comes to those incapable of volitional willful acts of sin, we can rest assured God will, indeed, do right. Precious little ones are the objects of His saving mercy and grace.

Conclusion:

On September 29, 1861, the great Baptist pastor, Charles Spurgeon, preached a message entitled "Infant Salvation." Spurgeon affirmed that God saved little ones without limitation and exception. As was his manner, he turned to conclude the message with an evangelistic appeal to parents who might be lost. Listen to his pleas:

"Many of you are parents who have children in Heaven. Is it not a desirable thing that you should be there too? And yet, have I not in these galleries and this are some, perhaps many, who have no hope hereafter? … Mother, unconverted mother, from the battlements of Heaven your child beckons you to Paradise. Father, ungodly, impenitent father, the little eyes that once looked joyously on you, look down upon you now and the lips which had scarcely learned to call you "Father" ere they were sealed by the silence of death, may be heard as with a still, small voice, saying to you this morning, "Father, must we be forever divided by the great gulf which no man can pass?" If you wilt, think of these matters, perhaps the heart will begin to move, and the eyes may begin to flow, and then may the Holy Spirit put before thine eyes the cross of the Savior … if thou wilt turn thine eye to Him, thou shalt live…"

Little ones are precious in God's sight. If they die, they go to Heaven. Parents, who have lost a little one, if they have trusted Jesus, can be confident of a wonderful reunion someday. Are you hopeful of seeing again that little treasure God entrusted to you for such a short time? Jesus has made a way. Come to Him now and someday you will see them again.

As I read their paper there is very little that I disagree with, but what I am suggesting may give more comfort to those that have lost a baby for any reason including abortion or miscarriage. In 1 John 2:2, "He (Jesus) is the atoning sacrifice for our sins, and not only for ours but also for the sins of the whole world."

I agree with number 3 from above that we are all sinners based on the original sin (Adam & Eve) and that there is a time when a person realizes that they have "actual sin" in their lives. The statement doesn't go far enough to explain this, so we are to just accept it on faith which I do but I think the scriptures go further. This statement talks about reaching the point of age of accountability, the realization of sin in your life.

I don't know when a person reaches the age of accountability only God knows. When they can understand that they have sinned, then they need to know that Jesus loves them and paid for their sins. John 3:16. For God so loved the world that he gave his only Son so that everyone who believes in Him will not perish but have eternal life. Jesus died for all, and it is that simple message that God wants you to believe. Come to Him with childlike faith. Luke 18:17, Mark 10:15.

So, all the babies, whether miscarried, aborted, or before attaining the age of accountability, and all those that are mentally incapable to understand what sin is, are protected by God's grace. All of them will be in Heaven waiting for their loved ones to arrive.

Now we should not get carried away and think that we do not have to carry the gospel to the world because their names are in the Book of Life (Calvin). It is our responsibility as Christ told us in Matthew 28 that we are to go and witness to the world. We do not know when someone will be saved and how many times that person will have the opportunity to accept the gospel call (I will discuss this in a later chapter). Christ sent his disciples out to bear witness and to spread the gospel. If we do not share or go then we miss out on the blessing of seeing someone saved and the blessing of sharing. We are sent to witness not sit on the pew or in the recliner and do nothing and let God do it all. By the way, he will send someone, and you not only miss the blessing here and now but also when you reach Heaven. You will miss the opportunity to have it listed under your name in the Book of Life.

I thank God for finding me as a child and that I responded at that time. I believe it becomes harder and harder as a person grows and gains knowledge. The world begins to influence their thinking and gets in the way of child-like faith. People start to try and prove the existence or the non-existence of God. The mind gets in the way and Satan begins to influence our lives and our choices. There is a tendency to rationalize their choices. Even as Christians, the devil influences us if we don't stay focused on God's will in our lives. The devil rules this world and will attack everyone at their weakest points, having you rationalize our choices which leads to other choices, and then on to other choices until we are backsliding or losing focus on God.

CHAPTER FOUR

OUR CHOICES

I don't have to tell you that we make choices almost every second of the day. You are choosing to read this or put it down. Hopefully, you keep reading. The absolute best decision to make in your life is to accept the call to Jesus as your personal savior and spend eternal life in Heaven. This is the only choice that means anything in life. You will either decide to accept Jesus or not, there is no in-between. If you do not choose Jesus, you chose Satan and Hell (separation from your creator) and suffering for eternity.

Whether you choose to become a Christian or not the choices in life do not change. Everyone will continue to make the same type of choices. The right choices can become easier to make as a Christian because of the help of the Holy Spirit in your life. Christians do not suddenly become perfect or ever will in this lifetime. There is a growing process called sanctification. Even as a Christian you chose to grow in your walk with

Christ or stay stagnant and let the devil keep you down by continuing to allow sin to control you.

I believe a lost person is approached by God a limited number of times with the opportunity to make the choice or answer the call to accept Jesus. Pharaoh had many chances just with Moses and Aaron. (Exodus 10) I do not know how many other times he may have had the opportunity to follow God before meeting with Moses. God finally turned his back on Pharaoh because he knew he would never accept his salvation. He hardened his heart.

We know many people that wait until their later years of life before they choose to accept Jesus. God is compassionate, merciful, forgiving, and loving and He does not want anyone to reject his Son. He will continue to seek you until you have hardened your heart beyond the ability to have faith in Him. You see this in the Old Testament of the Bible. God continues to tell the people to repent so he can bless them, some do but most of them and most of us today do not turn to Him in repentance. We choose to worship something else like money, fame, jobs, and the list goes on and on. The devil has a large list for you.

You or I do not know when your last opportunity to accept Jesus will be. God is slowly blotting out your name from the Book of Life. You do not want your name to be erased from the Book of Life. As I discussed in Chapter 2. Exodus 17:14, 32:33, Deuteronomy 9:14, 29:20, Psalms 69:28, Revelations 3:5.

Choices are important in our daily lives. We chose to turn right or left depending on where we are going. There are crossroads daily that require choices that will lead us to good or bad decisions. These choices are the same for the saved person and the lost person. The temptations are the same, lying, stealing, murder, sexual immorality, and idolatry. Sin progressively lures us into a deeper pursuit of an ever-greater sin or thrill (we think) without the awareness of the increasing cost to our lives. See the enclosed illustration.

When I was young, I was told you can't go dancing. Baptists don't do that…LOL You don't go to that show, you don't do this or that. It was a lot of don'ts without a lot of explanations, or it doesn't soak into our minds. The people were trying to build a fence around things that might cause you problems in the future. The Pharisees had built hundreds of laws around the 10 commandments (laws) God gave to them. The pastor Dr. Charles Stanley said, "**The mind is where the war goes on, you *can't* put junk in and expect good out. You can't watch the television for four hours and read the Bible for five minutes and win the war**". Motivational speaker and pastor John Maxwell said, "What you do today makes your tomorrow". Now that I have arrived at my older age it is apparent why I should not have done a lot of things I did while I was growing up. There are things in my brain that I can't unsee, things I can't forget, and the devil keeps bringing them to mind distracting me. Things I wish I hadn't said and done that can't be taken back or fixed, if you put bad stuff in your brain, you can't get good stuff out. They are part me I wish I did not have, that hinders me from worshiping Jesus and becoming the person I know he wants me to be. It is part of me that I can use to help others not make the same mistakes. If I could have listened not only to my parents, other Christians, and God and avoided these things I would be a much better person today. Please do not deceive yourself in thinking that because you are 40 or 70 years old you can control or can handle anything. You still can't unsee some things or at times lose self-control and make poor choices. Only with God's help can we overcome the temptations the devil puts in front of us. As Paul says it best in Romans 7:14-20 "We know that the law is spiritual; but I am unspiritual, sold as a slave to sin. I do not understand what I do. For what I want to do I do not do, but what I hate I do. And if I do what I do not want to do, I agree that the law is good. As it is, it is no longer I who do it, but it is sin living in me. For I know that good itself does not dwell on me, that is, in my sinful nature. I have the desire to do what is good, but I cannot carry it out. For I do not do the good I want to do, but the evil I do not want to do – this I keep on doing. Now if I do what I do not want to do, it is no longer I who do it, but it is sin living in me that does it."

I know God has forgiven me for what I have done and will do, but forgiving oneself is not as easy because you have Satan and his helpers reminding you of your mistakes. If the devil can get Paul to do what he doesn't want to do how much easier is it for the devil to get me to do what I don't want to do?

The worldly decision method is based on relativity – it is only your decision to say whether it is wrong or right, and it does not matter what anyone else or God says. This decision-making idea will lead to your destruction.

Our life is a highway that we are speeding down with intersections of choices and opportunities to go off in the wrong direction. Whether we are Christian or not. We are victims of our minds. We choose what we think about, we choose to turn and then there is another choice and another. They can keep leading us down a path that we should not go. Jesus is the plumb line that we need to draw close to. How straight is the path you are on? Which choices have you made? Our choices here have eternal consequences. Will you choose to accept the call to Jesus or not?

CHAPTER FIVE

THE HIGHWAYS WE TRAVEL

There is an illustration of the "Life's Highway" on page 35. So, I will explain the highway to you.

The first section is pre-birth. As discussed, this is where God knows you by name and you are listed in the Book of Life.

The second section is the time before you reach the age of accountability when you realize your actual sin. This is the time when you understand that you have sinned in your life. You know you have lied or something else that you have done wrong. There is a whole list of things that you know of, and I don't have to list them. Sin never leads to where God wants you to go. You can choose your sin, but you can't choose the consequences. If you are reading this and are thinking about what is sin? The Holy Spirit will convict you and you will know. If you ask yourself, is what I am about to do right or wrong then you probably know the answer is, it's wrong if you must ask yourself.

Once you have reached this age of accountability, then you will start down either the wide path or the narrow path. If you accept the call to Christ at that time, then you start on the narrow path. If you say no, then you are on the wide path. The wide path is where most people go or start. There is a warning in Jeremiah 31:21 "Set up road signs; put up guideposts. Take note of the highway, the road that you take."

If you chose the wide path, then you have let the devil stay in control. Proverbs 16:25 says there is a way that seems right to a man but in the end, it leads to death. (Separation from God for eternity). You may think you are in control, but sin controls your life. Proverbs 4:18 -19 says "But the way of the wicked is like deep darkness they do not know what makes them stumble." You are going through life with no sense of direction and wondering what is around the next corner. There is an emptiness you may feel that only God can fill. There are some very moral and good people on this path, but they are still lost because they have not accepted the call of the gift of Christ's sacrifice. Deuteronomy 29:19-20, Proverbs 29:1.

The narrow path with Christ in your life can have a dramatic effect on you. Especially if you are older when you accept the gift of salvation. It can change everything in your life. As an example, I had a father-in-law that was a long-haul truck driver and a tough individual. He was an alcoholic, and his language was not the best. He attended a funeral of a friend, and the preacher told the group if they continued like their friend, they all were going to Hell. My father-in-law decided to follow Christ a few months later. He stopped drinking and swearing that day. God gave Him a miracle that day. On the other hand, my life did not change much when I chose Jesus because I was 8 years old. You will notice in the illustration of the highway the different times along the path that people will cross over from the wide path to the narrow path. You are not able to go back and forth. Once we are in God's hands nothing can separate us, or God does not allow us to go back to the old way. Romans 8:37-39 "But in all these things we overwhelmingly conquer through Him who loved us. For I am convinced that neither death, nor life, nor angels, nor principalities, nor things present, not things to come, nor power, nor height, nor depth, nor any other created thing, will be able to separate us from the love of God, which is in Christ Jesus our Lord." So, nothing or no one, even yourself can take you out of God's hand.

You will notice that there is an early exit on the narrow path. So why is that? If God sees that you have become a worthless witness for Him, you are in danger of being taken from this life. You have gone so far from the path God has set for you that there is no return. I can attest to this. If you recall in my testimony that there was a time just after marriage that I was not on a good path. No one could tell that I was a Christian by my actions. I had drifted very far away from God. One night the Holy Spirit came to me with a warning that if I did not get back to the Lord and start to straighten my life out that I was in danger of seeing Him sooner than I wanted. It was a real enough vision or hearing that I knew I had to do something. Christians are the salt of the earth and if you lose the saltiness what good are you, as Christ said? Matthew 5:13. I praise God that he woke me up and I turned around.

I look back at this time when I drifted away from the Lord and asked why did this happen? It was because I had not matured in my Christian walk with the Lord (sanctification). I was still a baby in Christ. I did grow some during the next few years but still had a way to go to truly mature. During the next few years is when we lost our daughter and God used this to draw me even closer to Him. It has been a slow process of growth since that time, and I think I have a long way to go even today.

There are other times when things happened to me that God used to grow me. In 1992, I had an operation on my ankle and overdosed on morphine in the hospital. They had to revive me, which later made me realize how quickly you can lose your life and asked myself what I had accomplished for the Lord. In 2020 I had an experience with Covid.

Fifteen days in the hospital with five days in ICU. The nurses and doctors did not think I would recover, but God still had plans for me. We all have things in our lives that have happened which will either move us closer to God, or away from Him. Loss of friends and loved ones are some of the most difficult, but God is always there with His love and plan for our lives. His plan is not always the easiest thing to see at that time and we may never know the full reason for things that happen, but God knows, and we can rest in his plan for our life.

Many people get saved and do not grow spiritually. They stop going to church to praise God and fellowship with other believers because someone did something and they got mad at God. They are still baby Christians and don't know how to act. Paul told people in Corinth (I Corinthians 3:2) he was giving them the milk of the word not solid food because they could not consume it. After all, they were still babies in Christ. I Peter 2:2 says we need to long for the pure milk of the word, so that by it you may grow in respect to salvation. Taking a little course, or an emotional experience will not solve your problems or make you mature. There is only one way to grow as a Christian and it is so commonplace and ordinary, it is the daily activity of getting into God's word and prayer. We need to grow in our sanctification so we can better understand what God wants us to do and how we need to focus on Him and His word. In Proverbs 4:25-27 "let your eyes look straight ahead, fix your gaze directly before you. Make level paths for your feet and take only ways that are firm (and avoid the potholes on the highway). Do not swerve to the right or the left (or take an exit); keep your foot from evil".

God has lengthened a person's life also. He added 15 years to King Hezekiah in 2 Kings 20:6. We must repent and seek God to make this happen. In I Kings 21, we also see that King Ahab was at the point of death and he repented, and God extended his life. God may have extended my life after Covid. I certainly prayed and sought God while in the hospital. I recently heard this statement "If we truly believed that God would answer your prayer, then what would you pray".

Think about this example for you of Life's Highway. Say you start out heading east from Dallas Texas on US Highway 20. Starting represents being born and then moving east to the age of accountability (Texas-Louisiana state line).

So, you get to Shreveport, Louisiana and there is a choice, and intersection that can take you to US Highway 49 going south to meet US

Highway 10 going east. In this example, US Highway 49 represents the first call by the Holy Spirit to accept Jesus. This is just an example, and I am not saying Highway 10 is God's Highway "LOL". Let's say you stay on Highway 20, and you reach Jackson, Mississippi, you have another opportunity to head to Highway 10 down US Highway 55.

You get the idea that there are many opportunities to go between Highway 20 and Highway 10 just as there are many opportunities to accept the call to Jesus. You may even turn off going north and follow temptations far away from Hwy 20. You find yourself in Maine, you have made so many wrong choices that you don't think there is a way back or that God even cares for you. You know there is US Highway 95 that runs from Maine to US Highway 10 that you could travel. God may call you at the very last moment and you don't have to change a thing but accept his call just as the thief on the cross next to Jesus did.

You will see that the temptations are the same on both sides of the divide. We are all human and have all the same weaknesses. Paul lists a group of sins in Galatians 5:19 "The acts of the flesh are obvious: sexual immorality, impurity, and debauchery; idolatry and witchcraft; hatred, discord, jealousy, fits of rage, selfish ambition, dissensions, factions, and envy; drunkenness, orgies and the like." This is not a complete list, maybe the top fifteen.

This list is the same on both sides of the highway whether narrow or wide, whether saved or not. There are intersections that we come to in life that require these decisions to be made and the temptations start as small things and move to deeper sins for example desire moves to lust and leads down the path of adultery, promiscuity, and sexual immorality to perversion. It may take some length of time to move through this cycle of sin, but you can stop it at any time by turning to God for forgiveness and help.

The devil knows our weaknesses and attacks Christians even more. Those on the wide path are going in his direction so he and his helpers do not have to spend as much time trying to hurt or embarrass them. Although, many very moral and good people are on the wide path going to Hell and never make the only decision that matters by accepting Christ's gift. No one can be good enough to pay the price for the sin in their life, only Christ can do that. When we get to the end of our life, and no one knows when that will be, the only thing that matters is the choice you have made about the call to accept Jesus Christ. Either yes or no. Revelation 21:27 Nothing impure will ever enter it (Heaven), nor will anyone who does what is shameful or deceitful, but only those whose names are written in the Lamb's Book of Life.

In between the two lanes of the highway is the center median. It gets wider as you age. It is harder to move from the wide highway to the narrow highway, but it can be done. Christ makes it possible to crossover the median. It is only one-way. From wide to narrow no crossing back. God also does not allow you to go back and forth between the wide and the narrow paths. Hebrew 6:4 says "It is impossible for those who have once been enlightened, who have tasted the Heavenly gift, who have shared in the Holy Spirit, who have tasted the goodness of the word of God and the powers of the coming age and who have fallen away, to be brought back to repentance. To their loss, they are crucifying the Son of God all over again and subjecting Him to public disgrace." Meaning you can't be saved and lost and saved again, it is impossible. God will not allow this. This is where I was and when God said turn around or you will be coming home to me.

I have heard the "Life Highway" describe in two other ways.

Evangelist Billy Sunday describes it as a baseball game of life. God desires us to make progressive steps in our lives. Don't stay on each base too long or you become stagnant. The four bases are: First base is salvation. You can't steal first base you have to accept God's invitation. You might be the best hitter but if you never get to first base you can't score. Meaning you might do a lot of good stuff but that won't get you to first base. The second base is baptism and church membership.

Some people try to get to second base without going to first base, joining the church, and getting baptized but it takes you going to first base to truly get to second legally. The third base is Christian service, which we are all asked to do. Age doesn't matter and start where you are now. Home plate is Heaven, the reward for playing the game and finishing strong as Paul did.

Pastor Larry Adams explains it this way: there are five lanes in our lives. 1. The fast lane – people are always in a hurry like the prodigal son. He wanted his inheritance now and wasted it. 2. False Lane like King Belshazzar partying in Daniel 5. Going the wrong way and God gave Him a vision to correct his way. 3. Fools Lane is about a rich young ruler who made a foolish decision relying on his wealth. 4. Fear Lane where fear is mentioned 35 times in the Bible. Once for each day that leads to failure in your life. 5. Faith Lane as Paul tells Timothy in 2 Timothy 1:12 that God can guard what I have entrusted to Him until that day. The day he is called home to Heaven.

The results of the highway will be death, but which side of the median will you be on? The narrow road or the wide road?

So, we may be driving, walking, or playing baseball but the answer is God has a plan for each of our lives. The choices we make along the way impact our lives and determine the highway we are on, whether the wide or the narrow. It also determines the level of maturity we are as Christians. So, are you growing, stagnant, or moving backward as a Christian?

CHAPTER SIX

GOD'S WILL

I don't know what the specific will is for your life, but there are some things the Bible does tell us about our life and what is expected of a Christian. If you are not a Christian, then "God's Will" will be that you choose to accept the call to Jesus and become a Christian.

As a Christian, you should be on a path of sanctification. What does that mean? We are to be striving to be more like Christ each day. How do we do that? We should talk to God, read, and study his word, and do what he prompts us to do. Love the Lord with all our hearts, soul, and mind. Love our neighbors as ourselves. This is much easier said than done. The devil puts all kinds of things in our path, life, work, church work even. We get so busy we don't have time to study or pray we think. **Don't let the devil win!**

As a Christian, the world tries to tell us we should be perfect. They expect everyone to fix the economy, ecosystem, weather, wars, racism, and bullying. The problem is that we humans are not perfect, and the devil has full reign in this world and the only way to fix these problems is for Christ to return. We should try to do our very best to solve and work on these issues, not just give up. We should not stick our heads in the sand and ignore the issues of the world but know that God is in control and his plan will come to fruition.

Jeremiah preached for over 40 years trying to tell the people of Judah that Babylon was coming to judge them for their sins, but no one listened to him. Sure enough, God sent Babylon in to take over the land of Judah and put the people of God in captivity. God is in control, and you will not be able to stop his judgment if you do not repent and change your ways.

I have recently met several people that do not attend Church because they had a bad experience with some people in a church. Do not let the people of a church keep you from finding Christ. They are sinners like you and me and have all the same issues of pride, jealousy, etc. It is your decision to make concerning Jesus. There is a congregation for you if you know Jesus, keep looking. We all need others to help us grow and stay focused on God and His will for us.

A statement I read says "When the final day comes, if a man should find Himself in eternal damnation, he has no one to blame but Himself. Should he find Himself in the glorious eternity of Heaven, he has no one to thank but God!"

CHAPTER SEVEN

PREDESTINATION

What has been said about predestination in the past? In the dictionaries, it says, "You believe that people have no control over events because everything has already been decided by a power such as God or fate." Calvin uses this as a reason to do nothing because God has already predestined all of us. I have a slightly different take on predestination, a paradigm shift in thinking.

Let's take the same example as before, you start out heading east from Dallas Texas on US Highway 20. Starting represents being born and then moving east to the age of accountability. So, you get to Shreveport, Louisiana and there is a choice, and an intersection that can take you to US Highway 49 going south to meet US Highway 10 going east. In this example, US Highway 49 represents the first call by the Holy Spirit to accept Jesus. Both US Highway 20 and 10 go east and both highways end up at the Atlantic Ocean (eternity) but there are different predestinations for each highway. Highway 20 ends in South Carolina and Highway 10 ends in Florida. These highways both end in the Atlantic Ocean but at different locations. There is quite a divide between where they enter the ocean but they both end in the ocean or life's highway ends where eternity starts. If you are on the narrow highway (10) then you are predestined to be like Christ in eternity. If you chose the wide highway your predestination is Hell and separation from God. The choice of highway will determine your destination. Either in Heaven or Hell. Where do you want to spend eternity?

Can predestination be this simply explained? Maybe, but many scholars have argued about predestination for a long time. We know that God is omniscient (all-knowing) which means he knows what decisions we will make, and nothing surprises Him, but just because He knows does not mean He makes you make the decisions you do. I think many people believe that because God knows who will and will not accept the call that he is controlling them and their decisions, so he predestines them Himself.

God does things very simply many times. His salvation is easy, just have the faith of a child in Jesus. Can predestination be as simple? If you choose to accept the call to Jesus, then your name is permanently in the Book of Life and predestined to be like Christ when you get to Heaven. If you do not accept the call, then you are predestined to go to Hell and suffer the judgment of sin.

Let's look at some of the verses in the Bible that talk most directly about predestination.

Romans 8:28 "And we know that in all things God works for the good of those who love Him, who have been called according to his purpose. For those God foreknew he also predestined to be conformed to the image of his Son, that he might be the firstborn among many brothers and sisters. And those he predestined, he also called; those he called, he also justified; those he justified, he also glorified."

Ephesians 1: 4 For he chose us in Him before the creation of the world to be holy and blameless in his sight. In love, he predestined us for adoption to sonship through Jesus Christ, by his pleasure and will— to the praise of his glorious grace, which he has freely given us in the One he loves.

If we look at the wedding feast in Matthew 22. All were called to the feast but only a few came. One showed up but did not accept the gift of wedding clothing but was trying to attend as he was but got thrown out. So not everyone will accept the call, and some will try and sneak in without success. God will separate us at the opening of the books at the final judgment.

Can we apply Romans 8 verses to my stated theory? There are some assumptions to be made with the theory which are:

1. God wrote our names in the Book of Life at the creation of the world.

2. Since everyone's name is in the Book of Life, all are predestined to be like Christ at that time.

3. Everyone gets a call from the Holy Spirit and those that answer the call with a yes of acceptance will be saved. (Repenting of your sins) Romans 10:13.

4. Everyone that does not accept the call: Then you become in danger of being blotted out of the Book of Life. Rejecting the Holy Spirits' call is the only unforgivable sin. Mark 3:29

5. Once you have accepted the call, you are now on the road to being justified and thus glorified. The process of sanctification and maturity as a Christian.

God has predestined us to be like Christ only if we accept the call. We will only be like Him when we get to Heaven, and we are standing in his presence.

Just like US highways 10 and 20, the road of life contains many twists, turns, and exits. We often look to experts, friends, and even the internet to find help to navigate through the many choices. Does your

GPS lead you in the right direction? However, no matter what we do or where we look, we take far too many wrong turns. How quickly can our conversations, relationships, and thoughts be steered in the wrong direction? Our internal battles with sinful desires and wrong thinking seem constant. We certainly make our trek through life as sinners in need of a Savior. Where can we turn to find the right way to go? God always leads us on the right path, but His way is seldom easy or popular. However, God's way is always right. He can be trusted with what we cannot understand. Proverbs 3:5-6 "Trust in the Lord with all your heart and lean not on your own understanding; in all your ways submit to Him, and he will make your paths straight."

Let's look at one more scripture here regarding the paradigm shift: John 15 where Christ is talking about the vine and the branches. Much discussion has been about the branch that is cut off the vine. Was this branch saved or not? This branch as related to the proposed understanding is a person that is cut off because they reject the gift of Christ's sacrifice for salvation. They were listed at the beginning of the book but have been blotted out of the book because they rejected Jesus.

Some other passages and thoughts may change because of this new paradigm.

CHAPTER EIGHT

CONCLUSIONS

Life's highway is like our roads. Lots of exits, potholes, detours, and work zones along the way. We need help to make it through our lives. You can either have the Holy Spirit guiding you or the devil and his spirits showing you the way. It is your choice.

Be assured that I am still searching for the answers and growing in my sanctification and maturity with God. So, I am striving to be on the path described in 2 Peter 1:3-11 "His divine power has given us everything we need for a godly life through our knowledge of Him who called us by his glory and goodness. Through these he has given us his very great and precious promises, so that through them you may participate in the divine nature, having escaped the corruption in the world caused by evil desires. For this very reason, make every effort to add to your faith goodness; and to goodness, knowledge and to knowledge, self-control; and self-control/ perseverance; and perseverance, godliness; and godliness, mutual affection; and mutual affection, love. For if you possess these qualities in increasing measure, they will keep you from being ineffective and unproductive in your knowledge of our Lord Jesus Christ. But whoever does not have them is nearsighted and blind, forgetting that they have been cleansed from their past sins. Therefore, my brothers and sisters, make every effort to confirm your calling and election. For if you do these things, your will never stumble, and you will receive a rich welcome into the eternal kingdom of our Lord and Savior Jesus Christ."

I know nothing other than what God has said in His Word. This book is just the thoughts of a man. There are some things I know for sure, and they are:

1. God loves me and you and sent His Son to die and pay the price for our sins.
2. I will see my daughter Jennifer Renae when I get to Heaven.
3. God has a plan for our lives.
4. God is the creator, sovereign, and knows what is going to happen and the choices we will make in the future.
5. I can trust Him because He wants the best for me, even if I can't see it now.
6. God wants everyone to come to Him.

My hope for you today is that you make the choice today to accept his call. Also, this book has been a comfort to those that have lost a child because of a health issue, accident, abortion, or miscarriage, and those that have not been able to understand that there is sin in their lives.

Please email me with your responses and questions at lifeshwy10@ gmail.com.

REFERENCES

The Bible

New International Version

King James Version

And other versions

Nave's Topical Bible

Commentaries by J. Vernon McGee and others

Messages by Henry Spurgeon, Dr. Charles Stanley, and others

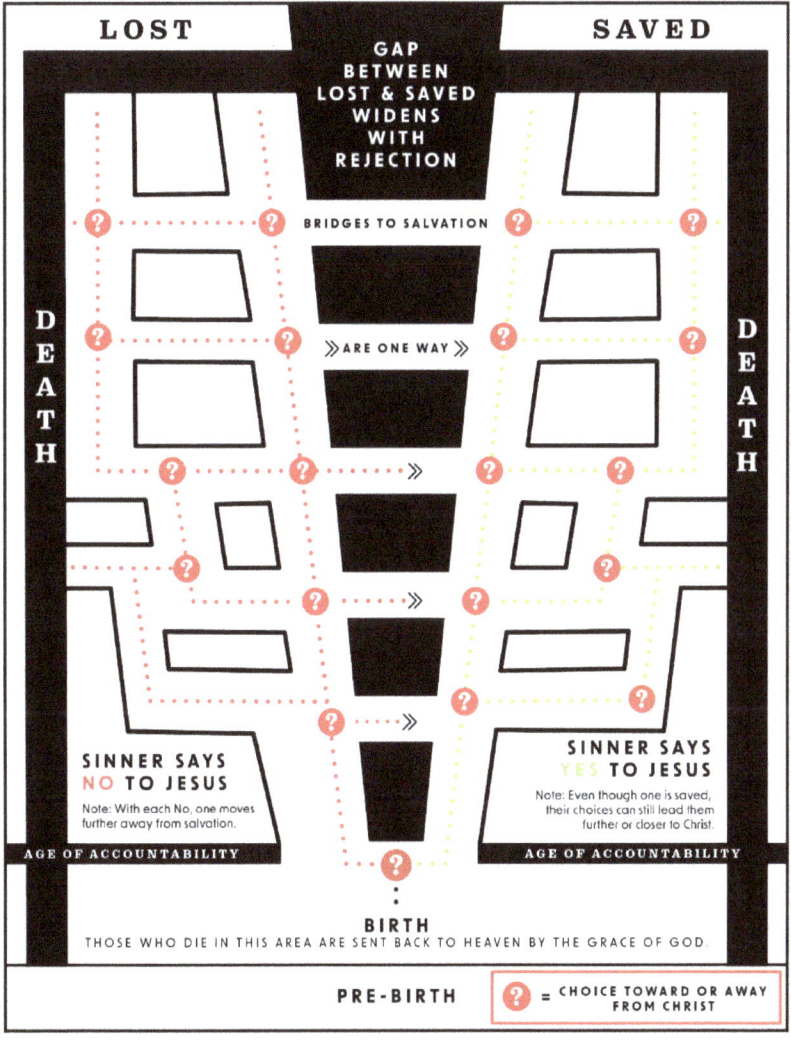

Family: Wife of 53 years, two sons, two daughters-in-law, and four grandchildren.

Religious: Has served as a church deacon for over 45 years and treasurer for 18 years. Teacher and leader of bible studies for over forty years. Two sons who are in church ministry.

Business Leadership / Operations: Founding partner of a manufacturing and service company. More than three decades of experience in senior management and executive positions at five companies, including responsibility for international operations.

Business Development: Designed and developed new products to be manufactured. Established and supervised the Technical Support Department for international operations. Established the first network of 2500 companies in all 50 states, Canada, Puerto Rico, Latin America, & Guam.

Environmental Affairs: Vice President of Sales, overseeing all aspects of environmental and sustainability policies and strategies, which include initiatives to address challenges like energy availability and security, raw material scarcity, human health, environmental safety, education, and development.

Finance: Vice President of Sales & Marketing with more than three decades of financial responsibility and experience.

Global Business / International Affairs: Created Marketing and Sales strategy with extensive international operations, including the ISO Sales System, and negotiated international contracts.

Community Economic Development: Partnered with a nonprofit raising over 1 million dollars to invest in businesses in third-world locations. Serve as President of a local Public School Foundation to support school district academic plan by engaging corporations and organizing fundraiser activities.

www.ingramcontent.com/pod-product-compliance
Lightning Source LLC
Chambersburg PA
CBHW051250120626
46547CB00014B/1874